WARS THAT CHANGED THE WORLD

CRUSADES

By Ken Hills
Illustrated by Francis Phillipps

CHERRYTREE BOOKS

The Holy Places

The city of Jerusalem and the Holy Land of Palestine lay at the eastern end of the Mediterranean Sea, where Israel and Jordan are today. It is an area sacred to people of three faiths – Judaism, Christianity and Islam.

Jews, Muslims and Christians made pilgrimages to Jerusalem and worshipped at its holy places. In the Middle Ages, Christians often believed that the places where holy people lived, the things that they used, and most of all their dead bodies, had miraculous powers that could heal the sick and bring salvation to the sinful. There were holy places scattered throughout Christian lands, but the Holy Land where Jesus had lived was the most sacred place of all.

Christian pilgrims enjoy their first glimpse of the Holy City of Jerusalem.

Christians and Muslims

Despite the huge distance, many pilgrims from Western Europe made the journey. Some travelled first to Rome, to visit the sacred places there, and then took ship from some Italian port to the Holy Land. Poorer people went on foot overland all the way. Pilgrims risked getting lost, being robbed or even murdered. Yet, every year, thousands of people made the journey.

During the Middle Ages, the Holy Land was held by Arabs of the Islamic faith who had captured Jerusalem and Palestine in AD 638. They allowed the Christians to come and go without hindrance. But in 1071, Turks, also of the Islamic faith, captured the Holy Land, and they were not so tolerant towards the visiting Christians. The result was a series of wars called crusades that lasted from 1095 to 1291.

SACRED CITY

There are many holy places in Jerusalem, for three religions hold it sacred to this day. To the Jews, it is the chief city of their ancient homeland, and the centre of their faith. It is sacred to the Muslims because they believe that their prophet Mohammed ascended to heaven from a rock in the heart of the city. Christians of all kinds revere it, for Jesus walked its streets with his disciples and died and was buried there before, they believe, ascending into heaven.

Byzantines and Turks

The Turks who captured Jerusalem from the Arabs in 1071 were determined to spread the Islamic faith and destroy Christianity. Pilgrimages from the west stopped. Only what remained of the Byzantine Empire lay between the Turks and the countries of Western Europe, and the Byzantine Empire was too weak to hold them back. In desperation, the Byzantine Emperor Alexius appealed to Pope Urban II in Rome for aid to fight the Turks and recover the Holy Land.

Christians Called to War

Pope Urban answered the emperor's plea with enthusiasm. In 1095, he ended a Council of Bishops at

Thousands came to hear what Pope Urban had to say. The cathedral at Clermont could not hold them all, so the meeting was held in a field outside the city gates. The crowd answered Urban's passionate call to fight the Turks with a great shout, "God wills it! God wills it!"

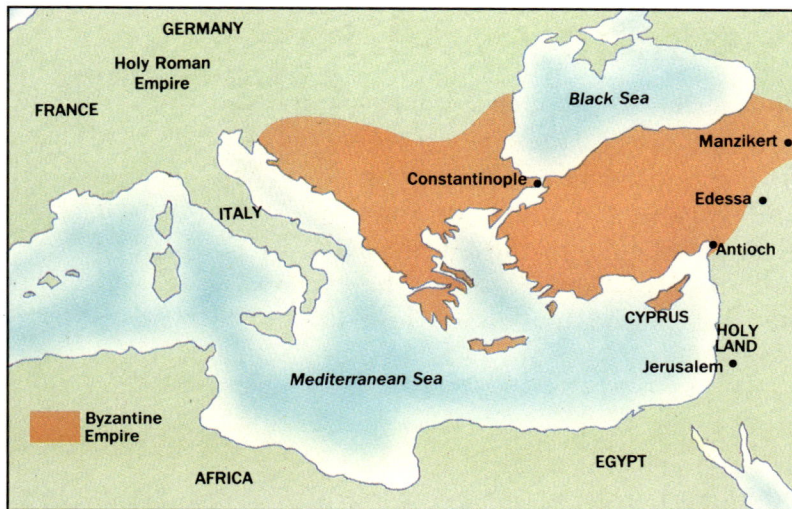

Map labels: GERMANY, Holy Roman Empire, FRANCE, Black Sea, Manzikert, Constantinople, Edessa, ITALY, Antioch, CYPRUS, HOLY LAND, Mediterranean Sea, Jerusalem, Byzantine Empire, AFRICA, EGYPT

CROSS OF CHRIST

The word crusader comes from the Spanish word cruzada which means marked with a cross. The crusades were to be wars of the cross, the symbol of Christianity. The new crusaders eagerly sewed crosses on to their clothing. People who went on crusade were said to have 'taken the cross'.

By the time of the crusades, the Byzantine Empire had shrunk in size, but it still protected Christian Europe from Arab, Turkish and other invaders.

Clermont in France with a call to Christians, rich or poor, to take up arms and drive out the heathen Turks.

Religious fervour spread through Europe. Pope Urban had promised his hearers that all who went on crusade would have their sins forgiven and go to heaven when they died. Armies gathered. Centuries of war were about to begin.

THE TWO EMPIRES

For centuries, the Romans ruled the known world. In the first few centuries AD, their power declined, and what remained of their empire was split into two, an eastern empire and a western empire. The western empire, which was made up mostly of what is now Germany, Italy and part of France, was called the Holy Roman Empire.

The eastern empire was made up of lands around the eastern Mediterranean and Black seas. Its capital was Constantinople (now Istanbul), a city on the Bosporus, the narrow stretch of water that joins the two seas and separates Europe from Asia. The empire took its name, the Byzantine Empire, from the city's former name Byzantium.

Both the Holy Roman Empire and the Byzantine Empire were Christian, though they belonged to different traditions. The Holy Roman Empire was ruled by German kings with allegiance to the pope in Rome. The Byzantines were loyal to their emperor rather than the pope. Today, their religion survives in the Eastern Orthodox Churches.

The People's Crusade

As the nobles of Europe prepared for the crusade, wandering preachers carried the pope's message to the ordinary people. One of these preachers, Peter the Hermit, so inspired his followers that many thousands joined him. They gathered in April 1096 in the German city of Cologne. These would-be crusaders were not the disciplined army the pope had intended. Some were beggars and thieves; most were poor, ignorant peasants, some with their entire families.

An Army of Robbers

In early summer, wearing their red crosses, this extraordinary assembly set off. Few had brought food or money. When they were not given what they needed by people on the way, they stole it. They attacked and looted a small town in Hungary and sacked the city of Belgrade. When they reached Constantinople (the renamed city of Byzantium) in July, they immediately began robbing houses on the outskirts. Emperor Alexius hastily arranged for his navy to ferry them across the Bosporus, where a Turkish army lay in wait.

Massacre

The crusaders settled down in a deserted fortress and immediately began to quarrel amongst themselves. A large group that set off to plunder the local countryside was trapped and wiped out by the Turks. When the main Turkish army approached, the crusaders foolishly streamed out to meet it. They were utterly defeated, with thousands killed. A few were kept and sold as slaves, a few more escaped and were rescued.

PETER THE HERMIT

Peter was a dumpy little middle-aged Frenchman. His face was long and gloomy, and he rode everywhere on a dejected-looking donkey. His feet and hands were filthy, as were his clothes. From top to toe, he stank.

Yet, to people of the time, these were sure signs of his holiness, and when Peter preached, thousands left everything to follow him.

The early crusaders went overland to Palestine because the ships of the time were too small and primitive to carry thousands of men and their supplies.

Peter's untrained and poorly-armed followers went into battle confident that God would give them victory. They were no match for the battle-hardened Turkish army, which slaughtered them without mercy.

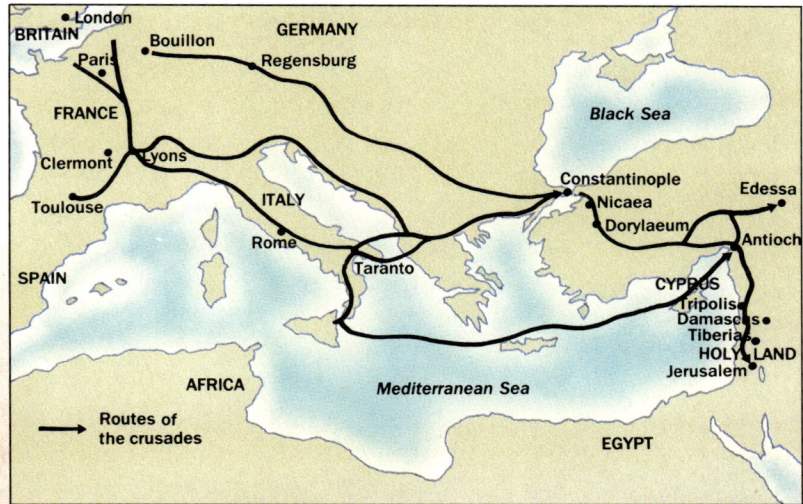

Map labels:
BRITAIN — London — Bouillon — GERMANY — Regensburg — Paris — FRANCE — Lyons — Black Sea — Clermont — ITALY — Constantinople — Edessa — Nicaea — Toulouse — Rome — Dorylaeum — Antioch — SPAIN — Taranto — CYPRUS — Tripolis — Damascus — Tiberias — HOLY LAND — Jerusalem — Mediterranean Sea — AFRICA — Routes of the crusades — EGYPT

The First Crusade

At the time of the crusades, the people of part of France were known as 'Franks'. Since most of those who 'took the cross' for the First Crusade were from France, the Muslims gave the name Franks to all crusaders, no matter where they came from. Three of the main leaders of the First Crusade were French: Godfrey of Bouillon, Count Raymond of Toulouse, and Robert, Duke of Normandy. A fourth was Bohemund of Tarento in Italy, and a fifth Count Robert of Flanders.

Jerusalem was a holy place to Christians and Muslims alike. The crusaders' brutal slaughter of the inhabitants ended any hope there might have been of the two religions agreeing to share the city peacefully between them. It made the Muslims as fanatically determined to drive the Christians out of the Holy Land as the Christians were to stay there.

The nobles of Europe who answered Pope Urban's call spent most of 1096 getting ready. In the autumn they set off, each leading a separate army. They met at Constantinople, and by April 1097 they had crossed the Bosporus. On their way to Antioch, they laid siege to the city of Nicaea, which fell without a fight, and defeated the waiting Turkish army at Dorylaeum.

The Siege of Antioch

Antioch commanded the way to the Holy Land, but the crusaders lacked the siege machines necessary to break through its high, thick walls. They camped round the city, hoping to starve it into submission while waiting for the siege equipment to arrive by sea. But they did not have to wait long. Antioch fell without a single major fight, for some Christians living there let the attackers in. Once inside, the crusaders sacked the city and massacred its inhabitants.

A few days later, a fresh Muslim army arrived and surrounded Antioch with the crusaders inside it. A year passed before the crusaders could break out and resume their march to Jerusalem.

Jerusalem

The crusaders arrived outside Jerusalem in June 1099. Their early attacks were easily beaten off. On 8 July, the Christian army fasted and prayed for victory. At dawn on 14 July, the main assault began. By noon the next day, the crusaders had scaled the walls and opened one of the gates. Those outside rushed in and the slaughter of the inhabitants began. In the Church of the Holy Sepulchre the crusaders knelt to thank God for victory. Outside, the streets ran with the blood of their victims.

The Kingdoms of Outremer

The crusaders called the conquered land 'Outremer', which means 'beyond the sea'. Most of the nobles and their followers returned to Europe, but some stayed on. The leaders of those who remained set up four crusader states in Outremer: Edessa, Antioch, Tripoli and Jerusalem. Godfrey of Bouillon gained the greatest prize, the Kingdom of Jerusalem.

The rank and file were given land in these new states. They settled among the Arabs, Turks, Greeks and Jews who lived there and gradually came to speak, dress and eat like the local people. But Outremer was never at peace. The Christians were constantly at war with their Muslim neighbours. They never controlled the countryside, for they lived in towns. Muslim bandits roamed the roads outside and robbed the pilgrims now flocking to Jerusalem.

The Templars and Hospitallers

To fight against the Muslim threat, certain Christian nobles formed associations called the Military Orders. The two most powerful of these were the Templars and the Hospitallers, named after the Temple and the Hospital of St John in Jerusalem, where both were founded. Members lived like monks, and fought like knights. They took religious vows and swore to wage unceasing war against the Turks. They watched over Outremer from their huge castles, and of all the Christians they were the most hated and feared by the Muslims.

Despite the efforts of the knights, years of warfare weakened the crusader kingdoms and in 1144 disaster befell them. On Christmas Eve, a Muslim army captured Edessa.

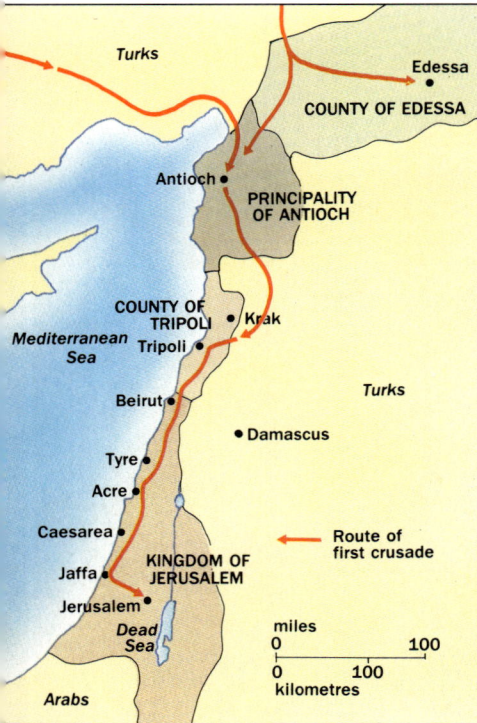

The crusader states that were established after the First Crusade were the County of Edessa, the County of Tripoli, the Principality of Antioch, and the Kingdom of Jerusalem. All around these states, the Muslims waited for revenge. When Edessa fell, the Turks were able to combine their armies and attack the long frontier of the other three states.

CRUSADER KNIGHTS AND CASTLES

The Knights of St John, the Knights Hospitallers, were originally just a religious order set up to help pilgrims on the way to Jerusalem. Later, they became fighters, rivalled only by the Knights Templars, another religious military order founded a century later.

The Knights became very powerful, and though they took personal vows of poverty, their orders were very rich. They built huge castles to dominate the land and overawe the people of Outremer.

The Teutonic Knights from Germany modelled themselves on the other two orders. Members of all three orders were renowned for their bravery.

One of the most magnificent of all crusader castles was Krak des Chevaliers. It took 30 years to build, and resisted every Muslim attack for over a century.

Krak des Chevaliers.

Knight Templar.

Knight of St John (The emblem is used to this day by the St John Ambulance Brigade.)

At Dorylaeum, Turkish horsemen bore down on the hapless German knights. The Turks wore light armour, carried small round shields, and their main weapon was a lightweight bow. Their speedy hit-and-run tactics outpaced the weighty Germans.

The Second Crusade

After the fall of Edessa, the Christians were in peril. In desperation, the rulers of the crusader states sent ambassadors to the pope in Rome, pleading for help to fight against the Turks, and to protect the Holy Places.

Pope Eugenius III took up their cause. He enlisted Bernard, Abbot of Clairvaux, the foremost churchman of the age, to appeal for a new crusade in Europe. Bernard responded whole-heartedly. Louis VII of France was a willing convert, but only the power of Bernard's preaching persuaded Conrad III of Germany, and his reluctant nobles, to take the cross.

Disgrace at Damascus

In 1147, the splendid armies assembled by the two kings marched across Europe to Constantinople. Conrad arrived first, and by October had crossed to Asia Minor and was on the road to the Holy Land. At Dorylaeum, a Turkish army pounced on Conrad's German army and utterly defeated it. Conrad, and the other survivors, crept back to Constantinople where the French were just setting off. Foolishly, Louis chose to go through enemy country in the depths of winter. The waiting Turks picked off great numbers of French on the way, and many more died of hunger or froze to death.

The remnants of the two armies met in the Holy Land the following summer, where more crusaders, fresh from Europe, joined them. With incredible folly, they decided to lay siege to Damascus, a city whose ruler might otherwise have been friendly to the Christians. They failed miserably. After five days of half-hearted attacks, the crusader armies gave up, and slunk off, back to Europe.

SAINT BERNARD

Bernard of Clairvaux was a French nobleman's son. He entered a monastery at the age of 22 and rose to become the most influential churchman of his time. The kings of France were his friends and Pope Eugenius had been his pupil. Bernard encouraged people to join the Second Crusade, not for the opportunity of fighting the Turks, but as a way to salvation. He was deeply distressed by its failure. Bernard wrote the rules which governed the Order of the Templars. He was made a saint in 1174, twenty years after his death.

The Rise of Saladin

Years of confusion followed the disastrous Second Crusade. The Christians quarrelled among themselves, but the Muslims made war on each other. For a time, the Christian states were able to survive because their enemies were divided.

Then a Muslim revival began. Nur ad-Din, governor of Aleppo, overcame the other Muslim rulers, one by one. In 1164, he sent an army to invade Egypt, by far the richest Muslim country of the time. The army commander took with him his nephew Saladin, a remarkable warrior. In 1169, when he was 31, Saladin was made governor of Egypt. He rose further, and after the death of Nur ad-Din and his son, became sultan of an empire that stretched from Egypt to Byzantium. Saladin now had a powerful army at his command and, in 1187, he invaded Outremer.

The Horns of Hattin

Saladin's army, 20,000 strong, captured the city of Tiberias, and besieged its castle. The Christians gathered the largest army they could, and marched to relieve it. The Muslim army waited for them at the village of Hattin, near a hill with two peaks that stood up like horns. A stretch of waterless desert lay between the armies, and the Christians rashly set out to cross it. They arrived exhausted, and in the battle that followed their army was destroyed.

The Capture of Jerusalem

One by one, the Christian fortresses fell to Saladin, and by September, his armies had surrounded Jerusalem. The few defenders were hopelessly outnumbered, and surrendered. On 2 October 1187, the Muslims entered Jerusalem and began to tear down the altars and crosses in the Holy Places.

The Third Crusade

The loss of Jerusalem shocked all Christians. Urged on by the pope, Europe's leading monarchs hastened to take the cross, but not until May 1189 did the first of the kings set off for the Holy Land. It was the largest army ever to go on crusade, and news of its coming greatly alarmed the Muslims of Palestine. But disaster overtook it, for its leader, the 70-year-old king of Germany, Frederick I (Barbarossa), was drowned crossing a river. Without Frederick's leadership, the splendid German army quickly broke up. Most went home, and only a few reached the Holy Land.

The next year Philip Augustus of France and Richard I of England set off on a joint crusade. Their two armies met in Sicily, where they spent the winter. In Spring 1191, they took ship for the port of Acre, to rescue a Christian army trapped there by Saladin's forces. Richard turned aside on the way to seize the island of Cyprus. Not until June did he land at Acre, to help the hard-pressed Christians.

The Fall of Acre

The weary Christians besieging Acre were themselves cut off by Saladin's army, but the coming of the French and the English gave them fresh hope. The newcomers built powerful catapults and tall siege-towers and with their aid made a series of fierce attacks on the walls of Acre. Saladin's men failed to drive them off, and the city's defenders lost heart. On 8 July, they surrendered, and the Christians marched in. Saladin withdrew and Philip Augustus returned to France, which left Richard in command of the Christian armies. He followed Saladin south, towards Jerusalem.

The 33-year-old Richard I arrives at Acre. He was a brilliant soldier, but too hot-headed to be a great statesman. His utter fearlessness in battle earned him the name of Lionheart!

RICHARD AND PHILIP

Richard of England and Philip Augustus of France led the Third Crusade, but it was not a happy partnership. Richard owned far more land in France than Philip did, and this caused bitter rivalry between them. They distrusted each other so much that they insisted on going on crusade together.

19

The Muslim knights were swift but they were no match for the crusaders in close combat. Their flimsy weapons could not pierce the Christians' armour, and they were easily unseated by crusaders' lances.

The Battle of Arsuf

Many Christians died of the heat as they marched, and more were killed in daily Muslim raids. At Arsuf, Saladin drew up his army across their way. His foot-soldiers attacked in waves, but their lightweight arrows and spears could not pierce the crusaders' thick padded armour. Then, with Richard at their head, the knights charged. They swept the Muslims off the field, and marched on towards Jerusalem.

Peace

The Muslims had been beaten but not destroyed at Arsuf. Saladin led them, in good order, back to Jerusalem while Richard set up his headquarters in the nearby port of Jaffa.

Saladin and Richard had by now developed a great respect for each other, and had begun to realise that a complete victory by either side was improbable. Saladin was weakened by illness, and Richard was anxious to get back to England where his brother John was plotting against him. In October 1191, envoys sent by the two monarchs began to discuss peace. Fighting continued despite the peace talks and, while Richard was away, Saladin captured Jaffa. Richard hurried back and, fighting at the head of his men, recaptured the city. Both sides were now weary of the struggle, and the talks resumed. In September 1192, Saladin and Richard signed a peace treaty, and Richard returned to England.

THE PEACE TREATY

The terms of the treaty between Richard and Saladin were to last for five years. They gave the Christians all the cities on the coast of Outremer as far south as Jaffa. Christian pilgrims could visit the Holy Places, and both Christians and Muslims could pass freely through each other's lands.

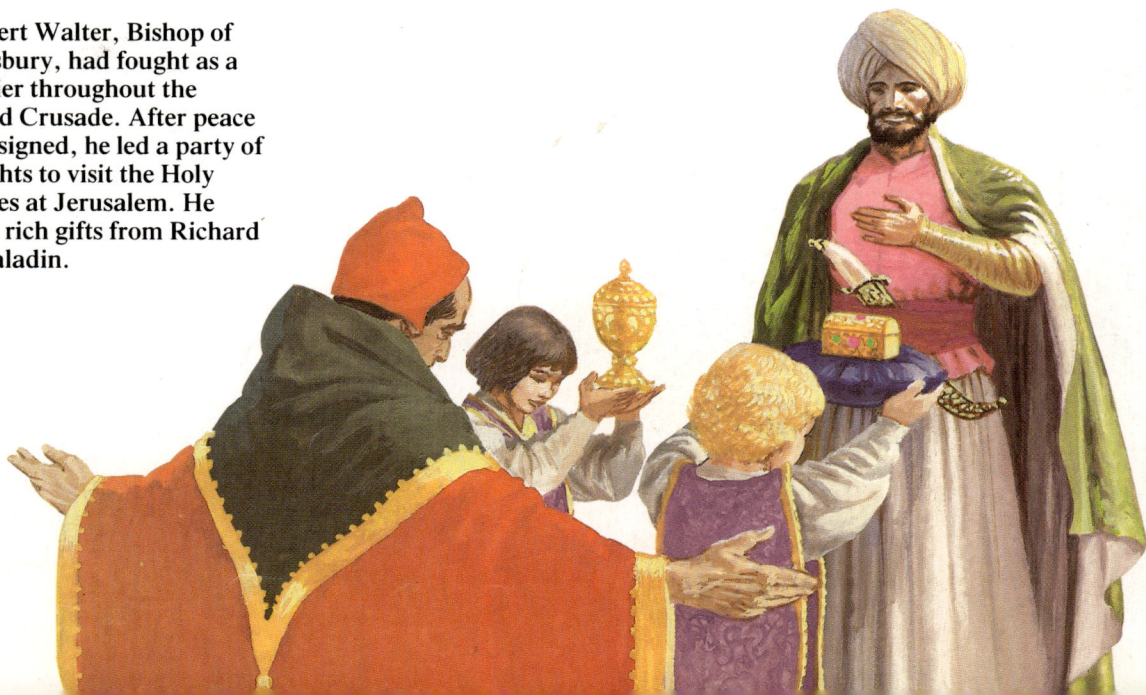

Hubert Walter, Bishop of Salisbury, had fought as a soldier throughout the Third Crusade. After peace was signed, he led a party of knights to visit the Holy Places at Jerusalem. He took rich gifts from Richard to Saladin.

The Fourth Crusade

In 1198, the new pope, Innocent III, called for a fresh crusade. The nobles who took the cross drew up a plan of campaign. Egypt was their first objective, for it was both the richest and also the weakest of the Muslim states.

Egypt could only be attacked from the sea, and only Venice could fit out a fleet large enough to transport the crusader army and its supplies. The Venetians agreed to hire out the ships but, as they did valuable trade with Egypt, they were unwilling to let Egypt be attacked. The crusaders owed the Venetians a huge sum for hiring the fleet. The Venetians suggested that they could raise the money by attacking and looting a wealthy city, and offered to help them. They went further and proposed that they and the crusaders should combine to capture Constantinople itself. The crusaders willingly agreed.

The wealth and splendour of Constantinople astonished the crusaders. The cathedral of Saint Sophia (now a mosque) was the largest and finest of its many great churches.

POPE INNOCENT III

Innocent III was elected pope in 1198 at the age of 37. His greatest ambitions were to reform and unite the Christian Church, and to recapture the Holy Land. A year after becoming pope, he preached the disastrous Fourth Crusade, which failed to reach the Holy Land and resulted in the sack of Constantinople and the wholesale massacre of its people. Innocent rebuked the crusaders savagely for their conduct. He died in 1216 while preaching a new crusade.

Nothing escaped the greed and fury of the crusaders and Venetians when they sacked Constantinople. An eyewitness said that no army in the history of the world had gained so much plunder.

The Sack of Constantinople

The Venetian fleet carrying the crusaders arrived off Constantinople in July 1203. The first attack was beaten off, so the crusaders withdrew and camped outside the city walls, while the fleet anchored in the harbour. The winter passed. Still the crusaders had no money to pay the Venetians what they owed, so they decided to try again to storm the city. The great attack was launched and met only feeble resistance. On 13 April 1204, the crusaders and the Venetians ran through the city, seizing everything of value and slaughtering the inhabitants.

The Children's Crusade

BLIND FAITH

In the Middle Ages, most Christians believed in miracles. Stephen, the shepherd boy who led the French children, promised that God would divide the sea so that they could walk to Jerusalem. Few disbelieved him.

In the summer of 1212, thousands of children, mostly from France and Germany, left their homes to go on crusade. Not one of them reached the Holy Land. The French group made for Marseilles, where a couple of villainous merchants offered them free passage to Palestine. Some were drowned in a storm at sea, the rest were sold as slaves. The German children went to Italy, but could get no farther. Without food or money, they had to beg to stay alive. Very few returned to their homes.

The French children went on crusade carrying the crimson banner of St Denis, the patron saint of France. Stephen, their leader, told King Philip that God had chosen children to recapture the Holy Land for Christ.

The Fifth Crusade

By autumn 1217, Christians from many European nations had gathered at Acre in Outremer for another attempt to regain the Holy Places. They planned to take Egypt first. With Egypt in their hands, all of southern Palestine, including Jerusalem, would fall without a struggle.

The door to Egypt was Damietta, a port at the mouth of the Nile. The crusaders took over a year to capture it, and spent even longer bickering among themselves before setting off up the Nile, into Egypt. Without realising the danger of it, they camped by the river where the enemy had only to open the floodgates to drown them all. The crusaders had no choice but to accept a humiliating peace, and to abandon Egypt. They had achieved absolutely nothing.

SAINT FRANCIS

Brother Francis of Assisi (later St Francis) came to the siege of Damietta on a one-man peace mission. He asked to be allowed to address the sultan, and crossed to the Muslim camp under a flag of truce. The sultan listened politely as Francis appealed to him to abandon his faith and become a Christian. As a sign of his respect for so holy a man, the sultan offered Francis rich gifts, which he refused. He was returned to the Christian camp with a guard of honour.

The Sixth and Seventh Crusades

The Sixth Crusade was led by Frederick II of Germany. He arrived in Outremer in 1228, but many Christians there refused to join him. Luckily for them, the Muslims were equally divided. Both sides preferred to talk, rather than fight. Negotiations lasted through the winter, but on 29 February 1229, terms were agreed. The Christians came off by far the better, for they regained Jerusalem and other Holy Places. Peace was signed to last for ten years. The crusade was Frederick's triumph. By clever bargaining he had won what years of war had failed to achieve.

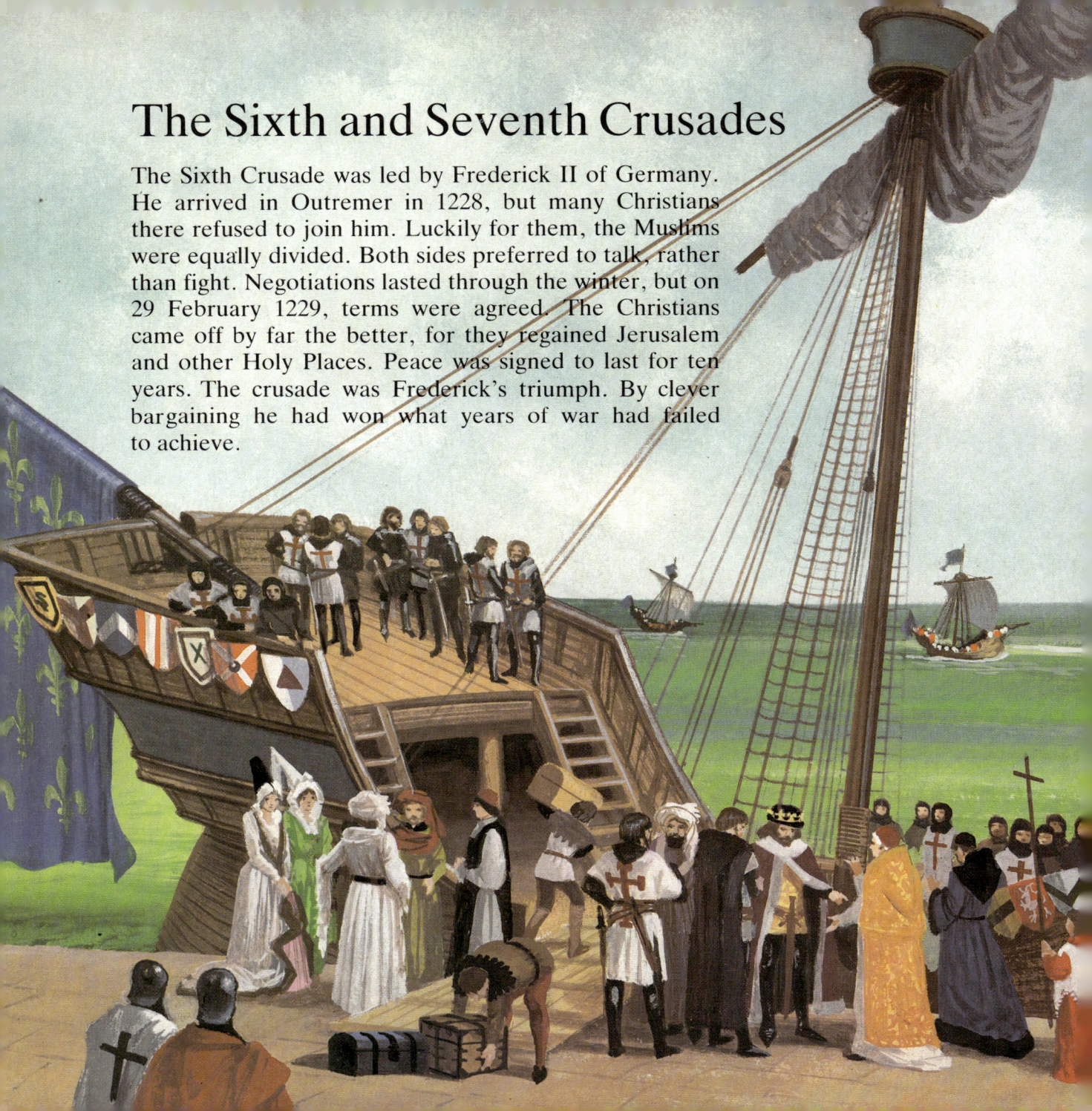

Frederick's gains were lost when in 1244 the Muslims drove the Christians from Jerusalem. A crusade to regain the city set out in 1248, led by Louis IX of France.

Louis attacked Egypt first, and Damietta fell without a fight. His army advanced cautiously up the Nile, but the Egyptians blockaded the river behind them and cut off all supplies. Food gave out and, weakened by hunger and disease, Louis and his entire army were surrounded and taken prisoner. He, and those of his nobles who had sufficient wealth to pay, were freed on payment of a huge ransom. The rest of his followers were executed, or sold into slavery.

Louis spent three years preparing for the crusade. He hired hundreds of ships to carry his army of 15,000 men, their horses and equipment.

The End of the Crusades

The Seventh Crusade ended in calamity, but worse was to come. In 1260, ten years after the defeat and capture of King Louis, a sultan came to power in Egypt who was to unite the Muslims and drive the Christians out of Outremer. His name was Baybars.

Baybars was a Mameluke, one of the elite band of warriors who formed the bodyguard of the Egyptian sultans. He was a fanatical Muslim, and as good a general as Saladin had been. One by one, the towns and strongholds of Outremer fell to him until only Tripoli and Acre remained in Christian hands. Baybars died in 1277. A truce between the two sides brought a lull in the fighting but, in 1289, the Muslims renewed their assaults on the surviving Christian fortresses. Swiftly they overwhelmed the port of Tripoli and closed in on Acre.

The Fall of Acre

The Muslims surrounding Acre outnumbered the defenders by five to one. Missiles from their great siege machines weakened the walls. On 18 May 1291, before dawn, the final assault began. By sunrise, the attackers were inside the city. By nightfall they were masters of Acre and of Outremer. A few Christians escaped by sea. The rest were slaughtered, or carried off to be sold as slaves in the markets of the East.

Crusading did not die after the catastrophe at Acre. The Christians of the West found other enemies to fight – the heathens of Prussia, and the Muslims of Spain. New crusades to Outremer were planned, but none ever reached Palestine. The dream of a Holy Land, safe for pilgrims and ruled by Christians was gone – for ever.

THE MAMELUKES

The Mamelukes were children from tribes in central Asia who were captured by the Muslims and trained as soldiers to serve in the sultan's bodyguard. They were taught Arabic and learned to become expert in all forms of warfare.

They were loyal servants so long as they were well rewarded, but in 1250 when the sultan promoted other favourites to his service, they rebelled and killed him. A line of Mamelukes succeeded him and they made Egypt the most powerful Muslim state.

The Christian defenders of Acre were massacred by the Mamelukes or sold into slavery.

The Results of the Crusades

The crusaders returned to their homes with a taste for the new luxuries and comforts they had found on their travels. Venice grew immensely wealthy by supplying the rising demand for these things from the rich and the ruling classes of Europe. The fall of Constantinople was a triumph for the Venetians, for it removed their main rival for the growing trade with the East.

The Calamity of the Crusades

In most ways, the crusades were a disaster. The crusaders failed to drive the Muslims out of the Holy Land, or to make the Holy Places safe for Christian pilgrims. Countless ordinary people, both Christian and Muslim, were persecuted, enslaved or murdered. The savage brutality shown by both sides, particularly towards helpless prisoners, led to fear and suspicion between Christians and Muslims. It has lasted for centuries, to the present day.

The merchants of Venice grew even richer as a result of the fall of Constantinople. Now they could trade freely with the East, procuring carpets and silks, spices and exotic fruits for sale to the West.

Important Events of the Crusades

First Crusade

1071 Turks destroy the Byzantine army at Manzikert.
Turks capture Jerusalem and stop Christian pilgrimages.

1095 Council of Clermont. Pope Urban preaches First Crusade.

1096 People's Crusade assembles.
Turks massacre People's army. First Crusade sets off.

1097 Turks defeated at Dorylaeum.
Crusaders capture Jerusalem.

1119 Foundation of the Templars.

Second Crusade

1144 Turks capture Edessa.

1146 Bernard of Clairvaux preaches the Second Crusade.

1147 Second Crusade sets off. Turks defeat German crusaders at Dorylaeum.

1148 Crusaders fail to take Damascus.
Second Crusade ends.

Third Crusade

1181 Saladin becomes sultan of Egypt.

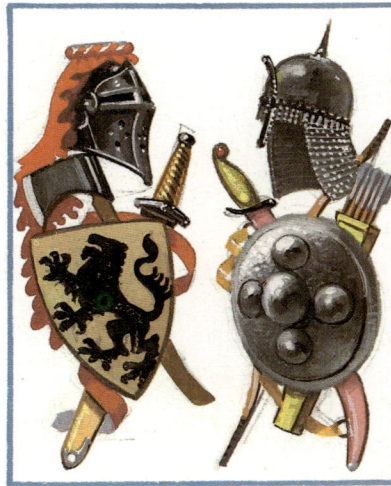

1187 Saladin invades Outremer.
Christian army destroyed at the battle of the Horns of Hattin.
Saladin captures Jerusalem.

1189 Frederick Barbarossa leads a German army on the Third Crusade.
Frederick Barbarossa drowned.

1190 Philip Augustus of France and Richard I of England go on crusade.

1191 Christians capture Acre. Richard defeats Saladin at Arsuf.

1192 Richard and Saladin sign a peace treaty. Richard leaves Outremer.

Fourth Crusade

1198 Innocent III becomes pope and preaches the Fourth Crusade.

1204 Crusaders capture and sack Constantinople.

1212 Children's Crusade.

Fifth Crusade

1217 Crusaders gather at Acre.

1221 Crusaders trapped on the Nile and forced to withdraw.

Sixth Crusade

1228 Frederick II of Germany arrives in Outremer.

1229 Frederick signs a treaty regaining Jerusalem and the Holy Places.

Seventh Crusade

1244 Muslims recapture Jerusalem.

1248 Louis IX of France leads crusade.

1250 Louis defeated and captured.

1291 The fall of Acre. The end of Christian rule in the Holy Land.

Index